# THE DARK LORD OF THE TIKI BAR

# THE DARK LORD OF THE TIKI BAR

Poems by

## Quincy R. Lehr

Measure Press
Evansville, Indiana

The text of this book is composed in Baskerville.
Composition by R.G.
Manufacturing by Ingram.


Lehr, Quincy R.
  The Dark Lord of the Tiki Bar / by Quincy R. Lehr — 1st ed.

  ISBN-13: 978-1-939574-11-4
  ISBN-10: 1-939574-11-0
  Library of Congress Control Number: 2015909070

Measure Press
526 S. Lincoln Park Dr.
Evansville, IN 47714
http://www.measurepress.com/measure/

Acknowledgments

The author wishes to thank the editors of the publications in which these poems have appeared, sometimes in slightly different forms.

*Angle:* "That I May Find Grace in Thy Sight"
*Barrow St.:* "Departures," "Maybe There Were Angels"
*Beans and Rice:* "Dizzy," "Blood"
*Birmingham Poetry Review:* "The Scottish Play"
*Clarion:* "If Love Will Seek Us Yet," "Shoreline"
*The Flea:* "Hopefuls"
*Kin:* "Seeds of the Storm"
*Measure:* "Sonnet on a Drugstore Receipt," "Avast!"
*The Moth:* "Like Blonde Girls Pray to Jesus"
*The Nervous Breakdown:* "In All the Great Terror"
*New Dublin Press:* "Postcard," "Blasphemy," "Increments"
*New World Writing:* "The Dark Lord of the Tiki Bar"
*Poetry Bus:* "Where's My Goddamn Bologna Sandwich?"
*The Rotary Dial:* "Climb Mount Niitaka," "Greatest Moments in Cougar Porn," "Left on Mission and Revenge," " Insomniac Lace-Curtain Shitkicker Blues," "Mouvement Collectif," "An Itching at the Thighs"
*Soundzine:* "Verdance"
*The Stinging Fly:* "Who Killed Bambi?" (Part I)
*Umbrella:* "Halfway Though a Latte"

"In All the Great Terror" also appeared in the *Census 3* anthology (Seven Towers, 2012). "Who Killed Bambi?" appeared in the chapbook *Shadows and Gifts* (Barefoot Muse Press, 2013). "Sonnet on a Drugstore Receipt" was a finalist for the Howard Nemerov Sonnet Prize in 2012. "The Secret Adventures of Carlos Danger" appeared on the *Mentioning the War* blog. "Where's My Goddamn Bologna Sandwich?" was inspired by a similarly titled song by Norman, Oklahoma, punk rock band Your Mom, and "Left on Mission and Revenge" takes its title from a Sisters of Mercy album that was never completed due to the breakup of that group's Hussey-Adams-Eldritch line-up.

# CONTENTS

This is the moment
when the pin has already hit the shell
but the bang is still in the ear,

when the note echoes
as the reverb swells
and the feedback goes from hum to hysteria.

~

This is the look
when the promise is unbroken,
but fingers brush together,

when the bartender nods
and begins reaching to pour
that last glass of whiskey you weren't having.

~

This is the prayer
when you know the request
but not the addressee,

when God, the Cosmos,
former and current lovers, dealers, mothers, fathers, and toys in cereal boxes
start to seem the same.

# Climb Mount Niitaka

It started as a blip, with scores of engines,
a constant, whirring blade, but multiplied.
Red sun and yellow blood, drawn by sounds
of all-night radio — a retribution,
shrapnel of industry cascading down,
another in a series of infamies,
a gambit coming from the wrong direction.
It's good guys, bad guys, greatest generations,
the lurid stuff of propaganda posters
lit by a molten shower of fire and lead,
the stratagems and counter-stratagems
of empire and empire, things that we believe
because we hit back harder.
                                        A cryptic whisper
crackles across the waves like poetry
or like a Zero's guns. "Climb Mount Niitaka . . . ."

# "That I May Find Grace in Thy Sight"

*All praise is to Allah, I'll fight any man, any animal. If*
*Jesus were here, I'd fight him too.*
— Mike Tyson

God loves an asshole — that was always clear.
The shyster second son who makes his way
from yet another swindle sees a host
of angels, yet he does not understand,
then spotting the deity, shifts to attack.
His fingers search for eyes, his teeth for ears,
and God Himself relents.
                              Why not just *ask*
and take what's given freely, nothing more,
waiting one's turn outside the tent or court
for a father's scorn or judge's reprimand?

(The families in the pew are murmuring songs
— contemporary setting — all-inclusive
Broadway knock-off, "multicultural"
Adult Contemporary. Beneath contempt.)

Why not accept the sound of a given name,
the order of precedence, the terms of bail,
the referee's decisions?
                              Greater still
the notion that submission comes from struggle,
the dislocated hip that will not stop
the match, the organ building its crescendo

in minor keys, an insolent demand
for blessing, landing like a punch or prayer.

# Verdance

The vision comes in fading light
like something settling in the gut,
an early bloom, a creeping blight.

The door that is or isn't shut
starts as a door, becomes a wall
smothered with ivy as the dusk
soaks through the trees. Under all
of this, one smells a treacly musk
that stains the nostrils with its scent:
a lie that we remain the same
(in flora fauna firmament).

This is our summer and our shame.
Everybody has their needs
in flesh and spirit — both are weak.
The garden's overgrown; the weeds
will find the thing they do not seek.

# Maybe There Were Angels

Concho belt and leather.
Long hair, off-center part
with bangs across my forehead.
Jesus' Sacred Heart
in all its tacky glory,
its post-iconic might.
Make sure to call your mother
and don't turn out the light.
Sometimes the river surges.
Sometimes the power's off.
Sometimes you'll say something.
Sometimes it's just a cough.
The sound comes in a murmur
mumbling for the word
for us and this condition —
the near side of absurd,
but in its antechamber
and slightly underslept.
Maybe there were angels.
Maybe Jesus wept.

# Who Killed Bambi?

*Don't ask us to attend cos we're not all there*
*Oh don't pretend cos I don't care*
*I don't believe illusions cos too much is real*
*So stop your cheap comment*
*Cos we know what we feel*
　　　　　　— The Sex Pistols, "Pretty Vacant"


I.
Carter and Callaghan and studio sets
decked out in cheap Formica, while the streets
reeked of garbage, as the long-odds bets
of older siblings came to nothing much,
their struggles syndicated as repeats.
Out of time and seeming out of touch,
the TV suits droned through the dinner hour.
Malaise. Hysteria. Declining power.

Yeah, blah blah blah. Who was really listening?
Shut your mouth. Shut up and hear me out.
Listen to my voice; I know its sound,
although I can't quite say what it's about.
Rain starts to fall. The putrid streets are glistening
as water takes the trash far underground.
It's briefly pretty — is *that* what I mean?
Purified somehow, but not pristine.

No matter what you smoke or — hell — inject,
the moment never *gets here*, just comes close,
looks in the door, sheepish, circumspect,
a bit embarrassed. Then it dissipates,

over in an instant at the most.
You try to find it in the dirty plates
and smoke-yellowed posters in your two-room flat,
but you've got memory — a wisp at that.

Put on your boots, break in the face you wear
until it's comfortable. Look for your lighter.
Affectations turn into addiction.
The skinny dreamer turns into a fighter
with curses on his lips and spiky hair.
Call it postmodern; call it contradiction —
neither's original, but both are true
images of what they did to you.


II.
It's not about the latest news;
it's not about your neighbor.
It's not the shirt you wear to work
or capital versus labor.

This is not your bedroom wall.
This is not your band,
the "vanguard of the working class,"
or program in command.

This is not your mom and dad.
This is not your school.
This is not the Iron Heel.
This is not a tool.

It's not about causality —
it's not the egg or chicken.
It's not the fuck who took your job
or who you put your dick in.

This is not a trophy case
of smashed-up, shattered glass.
This is not your one true love.
It's not a hallway pass.

This is not the evening news,
not music by Cheap Trick
for screaming girls at Budokan.
It's not your turgid prick.

It's not the song you meant to sing.
It's not the latest single,
Christmas carol, sermon hymn,
or advertising jingle.

This is not some freak-out show
hopped up on sex and pills
where everyone loves rock 'n' roll
and everyone gets killed.

This is just a desperate lunge,
a hill you need to climb,
a power chord that needs its fifth,
a phrase you need to rhyme.

It's not a bid to change the world.
It's not all that surprising.
It's not a phase of some great plan.
I'm only improvising.

III.
Somewhere between the gesture and the grasp,
somewhere between the titty and the asp,
somewhere between the cigarette and cancer,
somewhere between the pikeman and the lancer,

one hears the gunshot, doesn't see the face,
and sees the mother drop, the very space
transformed in her fall, the ground around her hexed.
The hunters are reloading, and he's next.

# Greatest Moments in Cougar Porn

If every poem has to do with love,
 then every video
concerns a neighboring desire,
 and all you need to know
comes down to similarities — a pulse
 that flickers into life
in front of a computer screen
 next to a sleeping wife.

Play with the thought of what you think she wants,
 a sequence of what-if.
Pretend her moans mean that she cares.
 Pretend you're really stiff,
and swear that she looks almost jailbait young
 (beneath the sheets, dim lights)
and that it's twenty years ago
 in more expensive tights.

But maybe it's the fib that feels like love,
 the lube beside the bed,
the unshared past conveyed in hints,
 the dyed hair on the head,
the fantasy behind the fantasy,
 the just reward of youth
with only wrinkles around the eyes
 hinting at the truth.

# Sonnet on a Drugstore Receipt

It feels as if there's something you should know,
something that I'd tell you if I could
articulate the thought, and it would make
all the difference. But comments go
through facile diagrams — each one is good
as sentence or paragraph, but doesn't slake
this hope for an alternate vocabulary
buried in my memory with stuff
like one-hit wonders, distance formulae,
and old addresses. Though I'm somewhat wary
and wonder if desire is quite enough
to justify itself or answer why,
I'll stammer my way toward words and hope you'll hear
the thing I'm trying to say, and that it's clear.

# Blood

*To be able to sing together*
*pulling the nets all together from the sea,*
*together to forge the iron like a lace,*
*all together to plough the soil,*
*to be able to eat the honey-filled figs together*
  *and to be able to say:*
    *everything but the cheek of the beloved*
      *we all share together*
    *everywhere*

*To achieve this,*
  *ten thousand heroes sacrificed their eight thousand.*
  — Nazım Hikmet, *The Epic of Sheikh Bedreddin*


Each empire must become itself, a thing
that ruptures like a half-healed wound,
a scab turned into blood again. It throbs,
but cleanly, shedding itself of pain, a rush
of faint, fanatic rage, a loss of blood
and trust in gentler prayers.

*Spread the news — a child is born*
*in manger or a ward*
*where all the parents look forlorn,*
*and the nurses all look bored.*

If God is love, and God's in each of us,
then God, too, can be spilled —
fish from a net onto a waiting boat,
a peasant's guts. *Observe the falling grain —*
it isn't that at all. It's loaves of bread

in kiln-like stoves, a janissary feast
in military mess-halls.
Fortunate orphans, uniformed marauders
no better than our own oppressors.

*Someone has to act the chief,*
*someone plays the squaw,*
*rich man, poor man, beggar man, thief,*
*the second quickest draw.*

There is no nation in my veins, no blood
in the pagan Christ hanging on the rood
— contorted face, emaciated ribs —
lean pickings in this time of want.
A stand-in, anyway, a lurid sectary
with washed-out eyes, a haggard face
implying a battle cry, a vote,
and glossy magazines with hatred in their headlines
and sleek Manhattan offices.

*Open the book, make sure to smile,*
*and start to read the lesson,*
*visualizing, all the while,*
*a stealthy make-out session.*

There is no money in my veins, no card
reducing me to a number, an ID
behind a four-digit password
that opens up my wrists like ATMs
— spewing like a casino jackpot —
an oil rig in the parched gray ground.
I won't be a transaction.

                              Never ask
what can or cannot be in numerals
if what's at stake is us, together.
The cost, if asked as such, will be too high.

*Another bill arrived today.*
*You calculate the cost*
*of everything you thought you'd need,*
*and what you thought you'd lost.*

If there is blood, Lord, let it be my own,
and if it must be spilled, then let the cause
be decent, at the least, and not a date
in someone's narrative that never was,
glory — or a shakedown for a loan.
Such is my prayer — I hope it's not too late.

# "In All the Great Terror"

*In all the signs and the wonders, which the LORD sent him*
*to do in the land of Egypt to Pharaoh, and to all his servants,*
*and to all his land, and in all that mighty hand, and in all*
*the great terror which Moses shewed in the sight of all Israel.*
— *Deuteronomy*, 34: 11-12

I.
Sometimes, I'd rather just forget it all,
that almost chemically pure fatigue
in feet and lungs and… nose. It was the smell,
that post-industrial residue of flesh,
burned paper, hard drives, staplers, pulverized
concrete, polyester-cotton blends
scorched to nothing, melted to a stench
that conjured all — and none — that I remember.

I used to keep the paper from the Tenth,
yellowed, crumpled from the trash, retrieved
like a lost letter from a distant home
that seems more real than this, and even now,
I can still hear the obsolete debates.
It's so far off. The Battle in Seattle?
Remember that? So many demonstrations —
in the end a brief, deceptive thaw.

Hardly Eden. Still, though, hardly *this*.
We didn't fall, but lost initiative
in toxic smoke — distant now as Heaven.
Something changed, and something had to give.
This is the public part. *And where were you*

*when the towers fell?* It doesn't matter
in the greater scheme of broadcast threats,
secret flights, and politicians' chatter.

Like hell it doesn't! Only scale divides
the micro from the macro, part from whole.
Metropole, periphery — each slides
into the piles of rubble, though one's role
varies — are you predator or prey
or passerby? Far off or far too near
or in the middle distance — either way,
there *was* a break, and it began right here.


II.
Beneath the raptor's eager eyes, the shapes of land
are laid out like a map,
the creatures crawling in the dirt look up and pray.
The long-expected trap
will soon snap shut in wings and beaks. His blood is up,
and he needs scant excuse
to turn at greater angles as he gyrates down.
No bargaining, no truce,
no lesser offers satiate his need to gorge,
and pleading is denied.
He jackknifes like a Stuka as he grazes ground.
Aloft again, his glide
is steady as his shadow sweeps across the plain,
majestic, proud, and fast.
He's headed somewhere distant as he flaps his wings —
but that's too good to last.
    The trains moved back and forth like worms beneath the ground,

and safely out of sight
of what moves though the sky, the tabloid headlines throbbed
through weak anemic light
in lurid colors, graphics bristling on the front
like paper porcupines,
and in the spectral, seated crowds, I strained to read
the threats in newsprint lines.
*Oy vey! Here goes another day!* But life went on
despite the evening news,
and train delays in rush hour set my teeth on edge.
One rarely gets to choose
one's useless fights or losing cause, and so I rode
my circuit as before,
emerged at 116th and Broadway at a run.
I muttered and I swore
under my breath through lectures and through snaking lines
in grocery stores at night,
through meals I microwaved and cigarettes I smoked
while trudging through the blight
New York in winter splattered on the city streets —
the faded, grayish glow
of streetlights shone on curtained windows, billboard signs,
and pellets of black snow.

   And on those lonely, late-night walks, I clutched my keys
and scurried like a bug
to read the paper once again when I got home.
Gratified and smug,
the president was smiling almost every day.
The opposition cooed
mild reservations. So it wasn't if, but when
a bully's chosen feud
would come to blows — but still, the monthly bills were paid,

and every curse I'd sneer
was matched with sighs and mantras that I told myself
no one would ever hear.
Defiance ebbed and resignation flowed, but still
I swore that I would fight
with words, at least, or aching feet when morning came,
but shudders late at night
proclaimed what we could not admit — not to ourselves —
no slogan-ridden shout
would save the creatures in the raptor's line of sight
or throw the bastards out.


III.
Invent a story and don't change the names
or worry if the images are stock —
it doesn't matter. Telling's the important part
in half-forgotten chants, in memories
like photographs are memories,
or songs… or like a long-suppressed lament
as distant as a saga, or as close
as languid anecdote. It's hard to tell.

Our plotlines come out piecemeal, episodes
of shows we hardly ever watch but see
on listless Fridays, know by reference
or catch-phrase — we despise them second-hand
or laugh at snippets, yawn as new clichés
assert themselves as truth. Accustomed order
rules each sentence — only for a while.
Pause for a moment. Take a breath, resume,

suspecting a digression, hoping it,
dreaming of a better narrative
subsuming this one. Speak it anyway,
until the fragments sag and finally give
way to the plot, or hint at it at least.
It's not the tale. Rather we want the voice,
the way it surges, stops, reformulates
between what seems inexorable . . . and choice?

Tonight, it's not dead generations' weight
that presses against my brain, instead two towers,
a story that I need to tell, though late
in year and politics — and in the hour.
It's almost muscle memory that forms each word,
recalls sensations I'd believed forgotten,
aspirations, touching and absurd,
and sentences more mothballed now than rotten.

IV.
And on the streets, 2003 would not replay
1968.
There were no barricades along Fifth Avenue.
The enemy shot straight
with laser guides and missiles and a satellite
and blats on infrared,
with snipers on the roofs and agents in the crowds
and choppers overhead,
with slick provocateurs on cable TV shows,
mendacities on air,
a rainbow spread of panic and a coded threat
behind a terror scare.

The grouplets quoted, formulated, and condensed
a bellowed politics
and combed the *Manifesto* for a perfect phrase,
a plan, an easy fix.
We scanned our books by lamplight, phrase by pithy phrase —
"But what would Trotsky do
if he were here?" We dug our mental trenches and
we took the longer view,
preparing for a surge, a push, a grand advance
regardless of the price
for just and fictive futures (maybe for revenge).
A leaflet's snarled advice
lay stacked on the kitchen table for a weekend march.
A sturdy pair of shoes
was by the bed, and leaflets sat in plastic bags
beside the monthly dues.
      And she and I were comrades first, and when we slept,
we did so back to back,
somnolent sentries snoring down the empty air
and braced for an attack.
But though her touch was cold and though she turned away,
I swore that things were grand,
her picket sign by mine outside the bedroom door,
a permanent last stand.
And through the fast-food meals I ate alone, I swore
there was no other way,
that soon enough the crowds would storm the palaces.
I smoked two packs a day
and paced the carpet in the living room at night.
I muttered to myself —
names and facts and parallels in history.
The books stacked on the shelf

were barbed with aphorisms, filled with figures. They
would prick my nascent doubt,
and life was great, with take-out pizza, dirty socks . . .
until she threw me out.
          But in the meetings and the vapid speeches flung
by speakers to the crowds,
the posture was defensive, bracing for the blow.
The thick midwinter clouds
were always present. Protest posters sagged and flowed.
The chilly moisture clawed
at slogans and at time and place, but still we fought
the rumored storms abroad.
          But how to fight? The opposition puckered up
and joined the frenzied cheers
while pleading chants of thousands in the winter wet
were banished from their ears.


V.
Pray, if you can pray, or fall asleep,
or stay up late with twenty-four-hour news,
scanning the ticker for the next attack,
or breach, perhaps. Volcanoes, hurricanes,
floods, new deployments, and rendition flights.
*We'll never be the same*, and never were.
A target is an opportunity —
we've always known this. Now we know too well.

The path of progress turned into a slog,
a forced march leading into God knows where,
a dull parade of hollow victories.
It doesn't matter what you think or do —

the radio shouts; the television's shrill;
the Internet takes what is blogged upon it;
and verse? There's always verse; anthologies
appear before they're pulped by the next disaster.

But still, somehow, I don't look at the scar
where, once, the towers stood when I buy ties
or compact discs or shoes. I know it's there,
but keep on moving and avert my eyes.
It's everything and nothing, simple loss
as unredressed as thwarted ignorance.
The cries for vengeance fade. Officials change.
The thing that stays with us is circumstance —

this mutilated city and the word
that seems to fit but doesn't or the threat
from outside or within, the way a bird
flies lower than before, though as of yet
it circles, but we know it has to land.
Call it premonition, call it fate,
conspiracy, or just a sleight-of-hand,
a warning that we all got wrong, too late.

# Blasphemy

*i.m. Thomas Bilney, John Tewkesbery, Richard Bayfield,*
*Thomas Dusgate, James Bainham, and Thomas Hitton*

The law is something in the eye,
perhaps a direction you can't look,
a destination when you die,
a way that human flesh can cook

for different laws, a different breach
than the mere lusts of greater men.
A man's imaginings can reach
Utopia; but still, a pen

is just a pen; the sword will trump
as scissors do to paper, slash
the bastard church into a rump —
but then there's rock. We hear the crash

against the metal. Paper's next,
then back to scissors. Hold your breath.
Stay inside. Don't mail your checks.
There's no clear trump in this but death.

Sometimes, the only way to fight
is at a remove, a proxy bout
with heavy bets each way. Despite
precautions, someone's still knocked out.

One can read it as one will —
mere violence, a core belief,

a martyrdom, or overkill,
a cause for sorrow or relief.

*Too late, of course — six corpses made*
*the arch-blasphemer's sacrifice,*
*the greatest law of all betrayed*
*as smoke rose up to paradise.*

# Left on Mission and Revenge

*For Tony, Marcel, and the rest of the gang*

Another greedy chancer
swears he's not the same.
Sartorially challenged,
politically tame,

all mouth and mission statement,
all circumstance and luck,
he makes you think of oldsters
still trying hard to fuck

but sadly out of K-Y
and sadly way off course,
beyond the Will to Power
or even use of force

to satisfy a tickle
with a furtive scratch
without becoming flaccid
or wondering what they'll catch.

Still waiting for a Savior —
or is it daily bread,
or maybe some aspiring
mouth to give him head? —

he fails to note his zipper
is firmly still in place —
a sin that never happened,
a voided fall from grace.

# Halfway through a Latte

I'm halfway through a latte, and I wonder
    when I'll feel awake,
the slightly nauseous pick-me-up,
    a muscle's fleeting quake
at nothing. Nothing for it. Not at all.
    The kick, as yet, is slight
and hasn't bashed the blurriness
    from the edge of sight.

Blame the markets. Blame the plutocrats.
    (That sound anachronistic?)
Blame the "state of world affairs."
    No, let's be realistic.
The bills are paid; I barely read the paper
    while sipping at the foam
that lightly frosts the paper cup.
    I should head on home

and drop the righteous act and just admit
    that I can't stop thinking
of you, despite the headlines' cries
    and endless coffee-drinking.
Or maybe it's your absence that creates
    these wan and sickly days,
those washed-out dreams, these aching joints,
    that dull, unfocused gaze

that only takes in shapes and blurs of color
    moving toward the door.
I try to blink away the haze.
    No luck. It's something more
than mere fatigue, or the sudden throb
    of the caffeine's swell.
Get up. Go home. I'll go away.
    I hope this finds you well.

# Insomniac Lace-Curtain Shitkicker Blues

One man needs to get a life.
One man likes to fuck his wife.
One man needs to "get a job."
One man's an expanding blob
oozing toward the TV set.
He hasn't changed the channel yet.
One man thinks he knows what's right.
One man can't quite sleep at night
but loses track, can't concentrate
on what it was he did, or ate
that keeps him up, his stomach clenched,
what word won't come, what thirst's unquenched.

# The Secret Adventures of Carlos Danger

*I start to fuck you so hard your tits almost hit you in the face.*
*You reach behind and spread your ass.*
— former congressman Anthony Weiner

Who is the incognito
    man behind the phone,
the shape made out of pixels,
    the bone that's not a bone?

You always liked a challenge
    and running up the score
and gave a both/and answer
    instead of either/or.

No Carmen Sandiego —
    the flag's beside the point.
Fire another rocket
    and roll another joint

as settlements, like roaches,
    crowd against a street
in multitudes, exploding
    in artificial heat —

a Palestinian village
    or mercenary dive
that lands you straight in prime-time.
    This thing is going live

like money shots on YouTube.
　　The leader grasps his rod
to satisfy a stranger,
　　enact the will of God,

and underneath the scepter,
　　danger is displaced.
A baby's born in London.
　　A leader is disgraced.

Whence the hooded axeman
　　as Henry's wretched freight
sent his wives' eyes wandering
　　towards men of lesser weight?

Where's Catherine in the saddle
　　or Caesar in his bed?
Where can we find a Borgia
　　to give us daily bread?

Carlos — you're more foolish
　　than even we suspect,
on Friday almost frisky,
　　the next day circumspect.

Another lucky lady
　　forlornly at your side
mouths pieties to newsmen.
　　The viewers will decide.

# Increments

Damnation rarely bursts out as a gasp
of recognition as it sees itself
smirk in the mirror, all sneer and shitbag grin
collapsing in a rising, cackling laugh.
We all know that we're really scum at heart —
but evil's something else . . . an avocation,
something that's as much work as being good.
We mostly feel too lazy for the big sins.
We stick to our adulteries, our binges,
small water-cooler power-plays at work,
a much-deleted browser history,
self-reassurances that if we know
we're being bad, it isn't quite so bad.
The dark and mutinous eyes that rise to meet
our pudgy, haggard faces only see
the increments and folds of slow collapse,
the cruel, sad forms that ultimately mean
nothing worse or better than ourselves.

# Postcard

A glint of sunset on a waterfront
largely devoid of ships — a blue expanse
of water and the same old famous skyline —
a scene that is and isn't what I want
to see tonight, or to experience
with seagulls, dogs, and joggers. Past the shoreline
of stunted plants and patchy grass, the water,
the closest thing to everywhere there is,
moves sluggishly away, its complement
of floating trash as well. And what's the matter
stays obvious, the linkage clear as this
impassibility, impediment
of miles of waves and storms sequestering
me from you, this land from everything.

# The Dark Lord
# of the Tiki Bar

I.
Landing. As the airplane ricochets
against the tarmac, he groans himself awake
and stares past fences, letting loose the thought
of a dark-haired girl he met — or thought he met —
tits jiggling as he took her from behind
(bodies generate humidity
that merges with the air despite the fan).
*Well, that was fucked!* he thinks. A fucked-up dream
of some entropic shithole far away,
a power vacuum with a city square
and old hotels still slightly redolent
of someone else's colony across
an ocean that's conveniently vast.
*Mistah Kurtz, he dead* — but in the end
if there's a runway, there's a way back home.

And this is home, a billboard sea of kitsch
along the access road — corrupted signs
and semiotics. Pad Thai. An English pub.
*Se habla Español.* You'll never find
a better deal on brand-new furniture!
He merges on the freeway, floors the pedal,
and penetrates the traffic, Cecil Rhodes
in Madras shorts seeking out a place
he sometimes likes to go — a tiki bar,

a relic of a previous century,
an old deployment, a beach bum on the Strand
hauling a metal detector. Fake grass roof.
Its Oriental peaks rise from the lot
and dominate the strip mall, while inside,
grinning humanoids carved out of wood
stare solemnly past tables of bamboo
and toward the sprawling bar. He saunters up
and orders a Mai Tai. *Let the games begin.*


II.
*Who's that behind the bar? Minor C. Keith*
    *or someone who would know*
*the way of the mixologist?*
    *These napkins need to go.*
*Their colors hint at hope. That's not the point.*
    *If anyone would come*
*for reasons besides the usual,*
    *they would soon succumb —*

*the strongest vows are broken over ethanol*
    *and a steady stream of spooge.*
*March on the guerilla road,*
    *end up another stooge*
*stuck drunk and stuck halfway across the world*
    *and through a credit line.*
*Repatriation's such a bitch.*
    *The cocktails, though, are fine.*

"Hungry Like the Wolf." *What time is lunch?*
    *Wake me if there's a fire.*

*Where can I find the central square,*
  *where a gun for hire?*
*Where did I put my damn safari hat*
  *that goes with my white suit,*
*the button-down that's on my back,*
  *the jackknife in my boot?*

*Who's the blond-haired guy with pop-star looks*
  *leading the camera crew?*
*I heard that they're all Limey queers;*
  *I know I've had a few,*
*but they're on coke (or so we peasants hear)*
  *and trying to live the dream*
*that's far away from offices,*
  *"there is no 'I' in 'team',"*

*and elevator music. Amateurs.*
  *Don't they know the drift*
*of how it works when the tourists leave*
  *and the waiters go off-shift?*
Another loser with a Section 8
  tries to drink it down
to where the fear's anaesthetized
  and unmoored from its noun.


III.
The figurine in brown might be a god
with anger lines in blue around his face
and a featureless gape of mouth. Across the bar,
his twin (or simulacrum) faces him.
A groan — equally inaudible —

contorts his mouth, a haka lodged like food
inside his wooden throat. No mere three days
mark this captivity. No Easter comes
with the last call. The muted god is trapped
within the silver Ray-Bans of a man.
He's sipping on a cocktail as his gaze
searches for a bit of tail but settles
on that gothic-looking dude with tats.

That guy's the real thing — he'll tell you so —
a "legendary muso" (aren't they all?),
an alcoholic junkie with a thing
for Adolf Hitler. *Much-misunderstood* . . . .
Well, *that* was fucked. But no one turns away
as he goes on . . . and on to Crowley now,
perhaps LaVey. *Chin-chin. Do what thou wilt.*
*I'll have another Zombie.* Left-hand path,
a roadmap of tattoos, apocalypse
in faded t-shirt and black skinny jeans
and albums out on iTunes.
                                        Never mind;
his is the least of cults, a minor league
of mere aesthetic malice — carnie crap.
Greater evils go by different names.

Just ask the Ray-Ban guy with thinning hair
if you can drink the courage — he should know.
His gaze is an abstraction — or a law
like gravity or entropy behind
the silver nullity. This is the stare
that napalms villages or beckons girls
with fondled dollar bills, that traps a god
within the concave mirrors of the eyes.

IV.

Drink up; this place is threatening to suck.
   The flash, ironic crowd
read about this in a guide.
   Jesus Christ, they're loud,
banal, and arriviste. Their lungs are pink;
   their teeth are straight and white,
the lesser sons of greater sires
   who rarely last the night.

You need to know the exits, note the crowd,
   and really case the room.
*You need to see muzzle flash,*
   *anticipate the boom.*
*The gooks'll get you otherwise . . .* old men,
   forgotten, off their meds,
are heroes of the later hours.
   The youngsters in their beds

and the piece of ass who flounces with their drinks
   don't understand the call
of all the booze within the juice.
   The knick-knacks on the wall
speak of *somewhere else*, a place recalled
   in flashback, more or less.
*Get us five clicks to the east.*
   Help us get to yes.

Help us now, you dotard, racist shits.
   The "Greatest Generation"
is laid up and on life support.
   Gen X is on vacation.

So that leaves you, the tedious Baby Boom,
   the hippie and the vet,
the taintstain of an empire
   that hasn't washed out yet.

We know your story, know it all too well;
   let's hear it once again.
What'll you cover up this time?
   What will you explain
to cover your ass or maybe to show off?
   *Those were the glory days.*
Don't you dare to skip your tab.
   Someone always pays.


V.
Consuela does the hula — half burlesque,
half pastiche Hawaiian, with a splash
of Carmen Miranda in the mix. She sighs.
One brown skin's like another. Veracruz
via East LA, she wound up here
despite her dreams. (Perhaps because of them?)
She longed to be a dancer, but shit happens,
tryouts get blown, and men can be such jerks.
Know what I mean? You take what you can get.
A gig's a gig; one dollar's like another —
even if it's cod Pacifica,
a fake grass skirt and bra, a dull routine
of thrusts and jiggles. Who'll call out the lie?
It isn't the performance, anyway —
no, that's unfair. It really kind of is,
but in the tits and ass. Of course they leer.

*Wanna sex my coochie, por favor?*
*Mi corazón es loco por amor.*

*You likee? Si? Then you can go to Hell!*
Some middle-aged white dude's staring at her boobs
behind the glimmer of his shades. She knows
his type. No, scratch that, she in fact knows *him*,
the workmanlike seduction, thin-lipped smile,
nondescript and moneyed, then it's back
to her place (he says, "Never take 'em home").
And even though she knows there's always no,
and she feels neither tenderness nor lust,
she knows she'll let him fuck her. (*That's fucked-up*,
she muses, *I never think I'm fucking* him.)
But someone always comes, and someone's sore,
and someone throws, and someone always drips
and watches the headlights fading as the car
turns to the road, a hulking exit ramp,
and then acceleration far away.

# The Scottish Play

There is a danger in the consummation,
ruin in vicarious fantasies
enacted on a stage, a supplication
offered to all the slights and injuries
that drive imagination to the point
of brutal eloquence, a lurid spot
that will not vanish. Legs break; a twisted joint
throbs with a pulse — blame it on the Scot.

All wrong, of course, since we don't fear, but hope
to sneer at the very thing that's self-inflicted —
greater than selfishness, a contradicted
impulse — where the point is not to cope
but rather yield, transcending one's desire
to feel the dagger's chill, to trip the wire.

# Hopefuls

I saw you through reflecting glass
    and lipstick smears of wine,
and even though drunk off my ass,
    I knew that you were mine.
And you were slender, circumspect,
    a grin that went ajar
between the Calvinists' elect
    and that prick Baudrillard.

We traded numbers (as one does)
    and staggered to the train,
fondling bits of pocket fuzz
    and mumbling to the rain —
a faded song, the chorus weak
    and warbled out of tune.
A kiss goodnight flicked past my cheek.
    I think I slept till noon,

dreaming about an old TV,
    an outsized golden cup —
and I saw you... and I saw me,
    perennial runners-up
exposed to unexpected glares
    of cameras and eyes
unseen but sensed. But I was there
    and scant feet from the prize.

*A thousand scared contestants*
  *are waiting for the chop.*
*The priests will don their vestments*
  *although it's only pop.*
*It's vapid, but I like it.*
  *Hear the critics groan.*
*Hoist the sail, then strike it.*
  *I don't think we're alone.*

# If Love Will Seek Us Yet

I.
A couple whispers in a restaurant,
and you and I can only guess the tone
of what they might be saying from the gaunt
wrist weighed down with bracelets she extends,
angrily flicking at a mobile phone.
He sighs, of course, resignedly pretends
he feels no panic. The menu's put aside —
so no dessert, a hurried denouement
of shotgunned wine and then the awkward slide
out to the streets, a hungry dog or cat,
an end they neither settle for nor want.
I watched — for the distraction? Was it that?

I strained at keeping them in line of sight,
a narrative that's similar enough
to you and me, the restless turns that might
twist your face toward mine — from separate beds,
the distance a relief, although it's rough
to search our dictionaries and our heads

for what we mean
in the yellow sheen
of a half-dead light bulb's glare
above a cluttered chair
and shelves and sheets and an unread book
and memories of how you look
when I no longer dream you, but you wait
not in sleep, but some adjacent state.

## II.

Somewhere, there's a man in love.
Somewhere, there's a habit —
a glass of wine, a cigarette
waiting for me to grab it.

Lips try to find the rising smoke.
The scents that thread the air
remind me of a ritual,
remind me of a prayer,

a smear of red against the lip —
holy, but a trickle.
A crumb of bread goes down the throat.
The way of flesh is fickle.

I'm not sure what the penance is
or if I should atone,
or if somebody's watching me,
or if I'm all alone,

and all the shadows that I see
are mine at different angles
in dim and inconsistent light
that both reveals and mangles.

Whose hand is that against my throat?
Whose elbow gives the prod?
Is this the bouncer on my back,
or am I wrestling God?

III.
To name a thing's to know it, to control
it in a way that's never specified
somewhere between the eardrum and the soul,
the strike and the reflex.
                    "Tell me if it hurts."
Tell me if it healed, or if it died.
Tell me what it's called, the just deserts,
a history that only lacks a name
on its front page.
                    And one commits in air
to the sounds that mean ourselves, the same
rustle of pages in an unread book
one hardly notices despite the bare
poverty of nouns to catch that look
you gave me. Let it linger . . . let it go,
needless and nameless, lost and out of breath!
Let it dissipate and sink below
memory's horizon, a phrase once chanted,
now mumbled sound, a useless shibboleth
hardly worth the entry it once granted.


IV.
There's always too much echo in my brain,
reverberations of a second thought,
and far too many figures — there's my age;
over there, you'll see the stuff I bought
for no good reason. There's the stain
from some forgotten sin. And there's the wage
I somehow earn that molders in the bank,
naming itself unto the very cent.

And there's her voice, still choked with love, still rank
and moldy from neglect. And there's a clock
that calls the time it was, and where it went
in whimpers of despondency and shock.


V.
You can count the inches of the light
expanding on the sill
this sleepless morning. All is blue
outside. No switch can kill,
even postpone the sun's indifferent rays,
redeem the fretted hours
of too-brief darkness. I can hear
the distant hiss of showers
and footsteps thumping somewhere overhead
to reach the distant street,
but I'll stay here despite the day.
It's best to know you're beat.

If I could rise and make my way outside,
if love will seek us yet,
if I could make it to the train,
and if my path were set,
I'd try to scan the shadows on the wall
of black or grayish tint
and graffiti on the tunnel walls
searching for a hint
within the whorls and wisps, a hidden map
of where I need to go
despite the hour, despite the odds.
I guess I'll never know.

VI.
We love you, ladies of the stratosphere,
and always have with awkward arrogance,
watching you spin uncaring through the clouds.
You must be there; I think I saw you once —
Did you smile? The vision wasn't clear.
The fog set in too soon in grime-gray shrouds.

We love you, ladies of the equinox,
and we return predictably to mourn
our wayward appetites, our listless lust,
another garment mended, then re-torn.
Was it sackcloth? Was it only socks?
See you again this time next year, we trust.

We love you, ladies of another place
with all your dances we don't understand,
your contrapuntal phrasings, and the bait
of features not our own. A different land,
season, and sky make a different face.
Is this *really* love? You'll have to wait.


VII.
Mother of incense, Mother of smoke,
Mother of the hour we croak,
Mother of mercy, Mother of peace,
Mother of wheels in need of grease,
Mother of glory, Mother of shit,
Mother of mouths around the tit,
Mother of wisdom. Mother knows best.
Grant me solace. Grant me rest.

# Departure

We always part in airplanes — up and down.
The "down" is always far away, and we
dress up for different climates, different times
of day and night — simultaneously.
It's nothing new, of course, as gray and brown
and green and yellow, dry and humid climes
remain sequestered. Only in the cold
of cyberspace, where pixilated glows
bring messages, as frigid as the snows
outside my door, are we together.
                                                    Old
or old*er*, anyway, I'm in a chair
of peeling plastic and bulging Styrofoam,
waiting for a disembodied voice
to call my row so I can get back "home."
I think of home a lot. The same dark hair
falls in my eyes. (I secretly rejoice
it isn't falling out.) But do I mean
my walk-up or that ranch house on the street
off Pickard Avenue, with yard and trees,
sun and heat and wet, allergic wheeze?
Do I move forward? Beat a quick retreat?
Do I make my fate or make a scene?
Regardless, I'm still stuck in LAX,
stuck with my face and sleep-deprived red eyes,
stuck with my memories, velocity
propelling me, once more, into the skies
to somewhere far away.

Smoldering wrecks,
Rorschach Tests of lust, epiphany,
and self-delusion, addictions long since kicked . . . .
All get jumbled up and in the way
of where I'm going or what I want to say.
Disused words recur. A bubble's pricked.

# Dizzy

Nothing could be worse than afternoons
spent in the sun, a city park of plants
in their genteel arrays. I can't sit down
or even notice them.
                              A lady swoons
in some far distant context; elegance
and ecstasy combine.
                              I'm back in town
and dizzy as blood rushes to my head
with images I can't make out — not yet.
They pulse and recombine and undulate,
alive as meat, quivering and red,
sensual, decaying — but still wet,
a parody of some more tender state.
Forget the grass's greenness — it's the heat
that drives us into frenzy . . . or retreat.

# Like Blonde Girls
# Pray to Jesus

Like blonde girls pray to Jesus, like a boy
    soon enough learns to spit
out bullets in a war crime scene
    when stranded in the Shit,
Heaven is where we thought it was, despite
    the wet, persistent swell
of garbage spilling from its cans,
    a rank and constant smell

of rutting, crapping dogs while luxury cars
    are mounted in the yard,
a trailer park on the edge of town
    beyond the boulevard
lined with shuttered stores and shattered lights
    and windswept, soaked debris.
This is the Kingdom meant for you,
    the respite meant for me.

This is the great communion — hobo wine
    left underneath a bridge
a quarter full and waterlogged
    as an abandoned fridge
gapes empty as a new-abandoned tomb
    in New Jerusalem.
This is the City on the Hill,
    the "us" of Us and Them.

# Mouvement Collectif

Elated, though I kind of feel like hell
on the 747 bus
winding through overpasses coiled as tight
as an electric magnet. Just as well
I'm leaving now. I might have stayed for years
in partial wish fulfillment, each of us
living in graffiti exile, fears
of new expensive jackets taking flight
like I am now, faithful, reluctantly,
to lease and love, to grocery bags and mail,
to bleatings of alarm clocks on my phone,
to staying off the pipe and out of jail,
to struggling toward the man I want to be
at home, with things to do, but not alone.

# Avast!

*Up against the wall, motherfucker! This is a stick-up.*
— Amiri Baraka

We cope through thoughts of vengeance, as the bulk
of suited shoulders, built linebacker thick,
fills the screen. Robotic baritones
bark out the boastful bigotries of empire —
battleships and credit lines and planes
over Tripoli. By land, by seven seas,
by God and the Marine Corps, Jefferson,
or some other fucker "with a funny name,"
another suited killer, they maintain
the weighted scale, the fixed rate of exchange.

But I imagine corsairs in the halls —
past the Chesapeake, up the Potomac,
then straight up Pennsylvania Avenue,
all turbans, cutlasses, and crescent flags,
salty curses shouted at frightened aides
as Barbary sets forth for its revenge.
"O say can you see?" Of course. The waterfront
is filled with ships, with rockets glaring red,

revealing tattered flags, sacked avenues,
the spoliation no one thought would come
though many had predicted it, and mansions,
miles of ugly mansions burning down,
a hinterland of suburbs caught on fire
as prisoners are whipped down to the quays.

# An Itching at the Thighs

Another day of news
or something like it —
Arabs versus Jews;
a deficit; a will to hike it,
and I'm staring past an empty plate
in some dump of a Brooklyn diner
in a fearful, furious state
of mind . . . where's the new one-liner
against the mute TV?
"Trust the president"? "Leave it to me"?

Outside a nearby store,
a boy has pissed himself,
drying urine caked against his legs.
His mother stocks a shelf
inside. It's just a little more
to go until the end of shift.
The man-child's gaze is stoic, but it begs
for sympathy. You get the drift.

That fuck in a sweater's speaking
a clutch of pious lies
on CNN. *Trousers leaking.*
*Itching at the thighs,*

and as that TV prick pontificates,
I see another face.
Dead Billy James Hargis howls

about the master race,
the commies, queers, and sundry hates
issuing from his jowls,

with different emissions late at night
out of his slime-pale prick,
the shame of every suck and bite,
the charges that can stick
like man to wife, like semen to a dress,
like a couple, each deflowered,
bewildered, trying hard to guess
where grace was lost, where Heaven glowered
like some abusive father/psychopath
with fickle love and life-denying wrath.

# Where's My Goddamn Bologna Sandwich?

*(With apologies to Maury Povich and Your Mom)*

It's not as if the meat itself
went bad like the credit rating,
withering like muscle tone
or like the girl you're "dating,"
the girl, you know, who won't shut up
and draws the eyes of strangers
like some slut in a sequined dress
or virgins guarding mangers.

It's something less than paranoid —
a case of misfired hunches
about a woman with ideas
who gives away your lunches.
Maybe it's something in your mind,
something emblematic
like smoldering bras in garbage cans
or letters in the attic.

*Where's my sandwich? All I want
is goddamn Oscar Mayer.*
Whose lips have tasted what was yours?
Who's the whore for hire?

So many hungers salivate.
So many tastes have shifted.
So many loves will go to shit.

So many meals have drifted
into someone else's mouth
and someone else's tummy.
The other guy is belching now.
You bet his lunch was yummy.

Pride can be a public wage,
even when you're beaten,
ugly, middle-aged, and poor.
It helps, though, if you've eaten.
The butt-end of the master race,
Before's deluded After
wants to know where his sandwich went
to disbelieving laughter.

*A real man knows what's goddamn his.*
*My sandwich, woman, boner!*
Who the hell do they think they are?
It's obvious you own her.

Sometimes it's gender, race, or class.
Sometimes it's slightly harder
to quantify the act of theft
or reconstruct the barter
from trails of crumbs or bleeped-out words
on daytime television.
Do we risk dialysis
or go for the incision?

Foaming, fuming, overweight,
you give the right impression
as the audience starts to boo.

Another easy lesson,
another creep who hates his girl,
who wants what he can squeeze —
fingers, necks, or mayonnaise.
The moral is a breeze.

*You're all a bunch of prostitutes.*
*You're all too fat or bony.*
*Call the station, call the cops —*
*but don't take my bologna.*

# Another TV Romance

I.
It's all just motes of light, mere chemistry
and physics, coalescing into shape
and voice and narrative, a different cast
and slightly different setting. But we see
each plot device and reminisce of past
episodes. On DVD or tape
or still in syndication, obsolete
titles and stars are frozen in the roles
that terminate as our remote controls
snap them away into oblivion
for some new hero, slick, urbane, and fun
as anyone can be seen from a slouch
with a bag of potato chips, a threadbare couch,
and her… and maybe me. I'm not quite sure
with this week's TV romance to endure.
Satellites, like angels on their pins,
dance around the world. Her show begins

with a premiere at eight.
The scheduling will help her keep it straight —
which emphasis of lust
will stroke the script this time, whom to trust
in the photogenic cast,
and if we're in the present or the past.
I don't know what to do.
She's sitting there transfixed. I can't get through.

A sitcom follows, sandwiching the news
of more austerity and further cuts,
of war and bombs, dissention in the pews
of dark gray churches. Then the laugher juts
from a set-up that we recognize,
a rerun recollected with a sigh
and all in the premise. Jokes get a backing track
— smiles on faces; malice in the eyes.
Again, the victim winces. So do I.
The punch line's like the night; it will come back.


II.
It must be in the jawline, in the set
of shoulders in a jacket, tailor-made
for some high office — note the notch lapels
cut neither wide nor narrow. You can bet
the cuffs are free of stains. Some shit just *sells*
every time commercials get replayed.

Not quite romantic; handsome, but only just —
he's Caesar's laurels on receding hair,
shoulder pads offsetting nascent girth.
Half used-car salesman, half a marble bust,
the pose is stiff but held for all it's worth.
The music swells, and we're supposed to care.


III.
*Good night, my dearest, if you understand*
*my thin, unscripted voice, the reflex quiver*
*I don't intend my tone to have, too high*

*to play the villain, perhaps a bit too bland*
*for leading roles.* I hope, though, there's a sliver
of an oblique charisma, so I try
to tell her that my feelings haven't changed
although the prime-time schedule's rearranged.

*Click.*

  Again, the episode's complete.
A job well done. Girls and whiskey neat.

*Click.*

  And *bang.* The villain takes a round.
Grimacing. Reverberating sound.

*Click.*

  And fanfare. Once again the news.
Famine. Rapine. Shrill opposing views.

*Click.*

  And pout. The model poses, struts
backstage. The cameras flash. The stage door shuts.

*Click.*

  A sudden silence as the room
is all there is at last. A sudden bloom
in different ambience within the ear
bursts out in varied hues, and all is clear

as she turns and looks my way,
noticing, until another day
brings another fucking show,
another plot with the same scenario

but with a different star.
We imagine this is what we are
as we lie down in bed.
Our dreams are similar but left unsaid —
implied adulteries
with people whom one doesn't know, but sees
beckoning luridly beyond the screen,
their lines the openers we come to mean.

# Seeds of the Storm

I.

I must have lost my accent years ago —
that's if I ever had it, twanging vowels,
slurred consonants — something I suppressed
between the tongue and teeth and throat and jowls
or simply lacked. I really don't quite know.
Was it a sense of shame still unredressed
but buried in rounder syllables? *How now,*
*brown cow?* No, wait! Or was it *rain in Spain?*
A misadventure on the Southern Plain
that lasted eighteen years? I don't know how,
but it's the case that when I say "again,"
it's a perfect rhyme with New York rain.

It's raining now, a constant pattering
against the window sill, and I recall
being caught out in flash thunderstorms at times
like this one — a strange elation as the fall
in barometric pressure, clattering
distant trains, cacophonies of chimes
on porches rearranged the very air
from molecule to macrocosm, fire
and water, every element, a gyre
of possible tornadoes. I would stare
into the churning clouds, past the spire
of some austere religion — loud and dire.

And every time I thought to pray,
I couldn't find the words to interact
with the dust in the air, the cough lodged in the throat,
the allergies twitching in the nose,
a thunder wall threatening to break into a sneeze,
sore-throat days spent in bed
until the weather turned,
indifferent to anything I asked or begged.
I never stood a chance — too delicate
in health and features to really look the part
of what we called success.
It's just as well, I guess.

And you'd stand off to one side; so would I,
staring with hopeless irony. We smirked
at where we came from, and we dared to wish,
at times, for something else. It never worked.
The pop chart hits got worse; the summer sky
turned even less forgiving, and so I left,
seeking the gray of clouds and concrete, cold
gusts of wind against my face, bereft
of home or even memory (I lied),
until I woke up, feeling, if not old,
aching and fatigued. I'll go outside —

I like the feel of movement, of the wind
blowing from elsewhere, a modest morning run
reminding me that just around the bend,
a few blocks further from the Southern sun,
isn't Utopia, but somewhere hidden
until one sees it, shaded and unbidden
and nothing special,

but I kept on running for years,
through bus terminals and airports,
large cities and small apartments,
past men yelling at women in Spanish
or construction workers in Polish,
and I found myself on a bridge

between two boroughs, staring past my feet
and through the empty leap and to the waves,
remembering, regardless of the street,
zip code, time zone, neighborhood, or town,
outward's not the only move — there's down
and even back. (I'm never going back,
not now or ever.) I somehow doubt I'll leap
or even turn around, although the crack
of thunder makes me think of you. Too late
for consolation, it's too late to weep
for what I never wanted quite enough,
for alternate scenarios in sleep
that give no waking solace. *Life is tough.*

The memories are hardly clear,
but come in a jumble of dirt and sunlight, red brick dorms
        and mobile home dealerships,
ersatz California blondes in the local team colors
downing farcically large numbers of Coors Lights on the
        lawns of sororities
while fat men in rusty pick-up trucks honk and bellow
as if it'll make any difference to anyone
in yet another endless summer of bad AOR and talk radio
        screamers,
of celebrity weathermen and country music blasting like
        the central air.

I try to explain it — even utter it
in some compelling way (who gives a shit)
in bars, in print, in everything between.
Can you, at least, intuit what I mean?


II.
Take a common phrase and mangle it
somewhere between one's memory and mouth
between the old impression and the thing itself,
between the West and South.

Beginnings of disintegration.
Sign lets go of sound.
The roots appear, gnarled and heavy,
from the eroding ground.
Song and saying dissociate.
The very sound waves strain
across the shorted wiring
of the switchboard of the brain.

Imagine how a bug might see the place
through many eyes, and wholly ignorant
of fragmentation in the retina,
not sound, not heat, not even in its brain,
a tiny ball of nerves, a battery
of fear and mute aggression,
                              unaware
that trying to hold this in a single sweep
of eyes and green and sunshine is the goal —
to synthesize what was in something else
than narrative, to see it in its shapes…

colliding, recombining, splitting up
in addled metastasis, illusory
appearances of fusion that soon break
into component parts when we awake
or sober up or go on growing old.

I should just let this go and act my age,
but that overripeness in that summer yard
hasn't aged itself, and if I screw
my eyes to squints, the hard
twinkles of back-porch lights cut through the husks
of plants, cicadas, nameless rotting matter,
wordless dream impressions,
and an overlay of wordless insect chatter.


III.
And this is the time that was, the interstitial
mess of train schedules, demands of course catalogues,
and the usual tangle of airport terminals,

and I'm skimming some bestseller
with one eye grazing the departure times,
waiting for the moment
when I can stop kidding myself
about the hopelessly gushing paperbacks
where love conquers something or another,
books that I'll never buy but gaze at
in boredom and disdain.

And we both know the aftermath of that
illusive final page — the moment where

one looks across the pillow at who's there.
The numbers don't balance; someone smells a rat,
and we wind up in bed with an alarm
set early,
           shuddering as light streams in
the smudged, indifferent window, blurred and thin
as a shaky laser beam that does no harm
but just illuminates the gathered stuff
on shelves, in drawers, in stacks, and on the bed,
posing whether this is quite enough —
accumulated words and sounds and pictures —
accumulated dreams that others had instead
of us — fleeting as morning, dour as the Scriptures
I can't un-memorize.
              The Holy Ghost
becomes another figment, just a wisp
of air recalling words, and at the most,
it's semiotics whispered in a lisp.

*Do you recall a half-lit parking lot,*
*dilated pupils — blue stared into brown,*
*does* that *stir a thing?* Of course it does!
Another tale of my reserves being shot,
another tendril from that goddamn town
drifting out, even now. What never was
should never haunt me — but the humid air's
vague perfume of gasoline remains
within my nostrils, and your shadow stains
a long-junked car like red wine on a sleeve.
We kissed a moment, then I had to leave.

Tonight, I feel... I wouldn't say regret,
but rather something I would not release
and carried with me — I could not forget
the timbre of your voice, though I found peace
with others — time here, time there,
other scraps of verse and greater tragedies,
sardonic jokes and hangovers,
close-packed boxes and storage units,
and, at times, a slight nagging sensation
of assignations permanently missed.


IV.
What's the word I'm hoping to convey?
Where's the past I'm hoping to relive
— not to change but understand *today*?
What's the wrong I'm hoping you'll forgive?
What's the mathematics of *too late*,
addition and subtraction, how a friend
is added or expunged? How long the wait
until the Reagan years come to an end?

And I always think I'm back in the grocery store,
walking my way through aisles of Cheerios, ravioli, milk,
dog food, cat litter, apples, various kinds of tropical fruit,
and childproof bottles of Tylenol,
and I'm always losing my mother,
always trying not to cry again
or throw myself on the bewildered mercy
of teenagers in ill-fitting uniforms.
Outside, black asphalt
stretches like some desolate pond,

beyond which and down a creek-bisected road
is the house
I still imagine as if in chilly haze
in some sleep-deprived morning
at the end of a holiday
just before the start of another semester.

Another cup of coffee gets me through
another morning, a nippy walk to work,
serenaded by the sounds of whining horns,
the clanking of construction, and the swish
of distant jets above — heading where
I almost wish I was — *I won't go back.*

*It's only foliage.* Remind myself
of that. The riotous spread of leaves
and shadow threatens to engulf the street
near dusk.
        I know the place too well,
each branch and root and twig, each prurient thought
mused many years ago upon that spot.

*I dreamed it all back then and hoped it true.*
*Did I recall your face, or was it more,*
*a fantasy, voluptuous and green,*
*a never-ending summer, me and you*
*or someone like you, just behind the screen*
*of a backyard porch, perhaps behind your door?*

# Shoreline

You pause a moment, sitting still at last,
and only feel a breeze and sun — hot, cold
in equipoise as you take in the sight
of shores and waves and houses on a ridge.
Our world is land and air, an island set
in amniotic possibility.
You close your eyes. You never liked the sea.

## The Author

Quincy R. Lehr is the author of three chapbooks — *William Montgomery* (2006), *William Montgomery's Guide to New York City* (2008), and *Shadows and Gifts* (2013) — and three full-length books of poetry — *Across the Grid of Streets* (2008), *Obscure Classics of English Progressive Rock* (2012), and *Heimat* (2014). His poetry and criticism appear widely in North America, Europe, and Australia, and he is the associate editor of *The Raintown Review*. He lives in Brooklyn, where he teaches history.

www.ingramcontent.com/pod-product-compliance
Lightning Source LLC
Chambersburg PA
CBHW030756150426
42813CB00068B/3176/J